Stand Out

Reading & Writing Challenge

Rob Jenkins • Staci Sabbagh Johnson

THOMSON
HEINLE

Australia • Canada • Mexico • Singapore • Spain • United Kingdom • United States

Stand Out 1
Reading & Writing Challenge
Rob Jenkins • Staci Sabbagh Johnson

Publisher, Adult and Academic ESL: *James W. Brown*
Senior Acquisitions Editor: *Sherrise Roehr*
Director of Product Development: *Anita Raducanu*
Developmental Editor: *Tom Jefferies*
Editorial Assistant: *Katherine Reilly*
Director of Product Marketing: *Amy Mabley*
Senior Field Marketing Manager: *Donna Lee Kennedy*
Product Marketing Manager: *Laura Needham*
Director, Global ESL Training & Development: *Evelyn Nelson*
Senior Production Editor: *Maryellen Killeen*
Senior Manufacturing Coordinator: *Mary Beth Hennebury*
Photo Researcher: *Melissa Goodrum*
Project Manager: *Tünde A. Dewey*
Compositor: *Pre-Press Company, Inc.*
Printer: *Malloy Lithography*
Cover Designer: *Rotunda Design*
Illustrators: *Ray Medici*
   James Edwards, represented by Sheryl Beranbaum
   Scott MacNeill

Printed in the United States of America.
1 2 3 4 5 6 7 8 9 10 09 08 07 06 05

For more information, contact Thomson Heinle, 25 Thomson Place, Boston, MA 02210 USA, or you can visit our Internet site at elt.thomson.com

Library of Congress Control Number 2005928923
ISBN: 1-4130-0721-X
ISE ISBN: 1-4130-2093-3 International Student Edition

CONTENTS

TO THE TEACHER

About *Stand Out: Standards-Based Learning*

The *Stand Out* series includes a five-level basal series for ESL learners designed to facilitate active learning, while challenging students to build a nurturing and effective learning community.

About *Stand Out Reading & Writing Challenge*

Stand Out Reading & Writing Challenge was written to give students additional practice in vocabulary, reading, and writing, while focusing students' attention on life-skill content.

Stand Out Reading & Writing Challenge is aligned with the basal series and is divided into eight distinct units, mirroring competency areas most useful to newcomers. These areas are outlined in CASAS assessment programs and different state model standards for adults.

No prior content knowledge is required to use *Stand Out Reading & Writing Challenge*. However, students will need the skill background necessary for their particular level. The books can be used as a supplemental component to *Stand Out* or as a stand-alone text.

Philosophy of *Stand Out Reading & Writing Challenge*

Stand Out Reading & Writing Challenge is intended for ESL students who need more practice with vocabulary, reading, and writing than they are given in most basal texts. Each unit takes students from a life-skill activity to vocabulary and reading practice and eventually to a finished piece of writing with the philosophy that students learn best when actively engaged in activities that relate to their personal lives and move from what they already know to new information.

Organization of *Stand Out Reading & Writing Challenge*

Stand Out Reading & Writing Challenge challenges students to develop their vocabulary, reading, and writing skills through eight unique units. Each unit includes a mix of activity types and caters to students with different learning styles.

▶ **Life-Skill Activity** Each unit opens with a life-skill activity designed to activate students' prior knowledge about the topic and prepare them for the following activities.

▶ **Vocabulary** Students are introduced to vocabulary that they need to better understand the reading. They will go through a series of activities designed to make them more familiar with the vocabulary and how it will be used. The lower levels use a variety of pictures to demonstrate much of the vocabulary. The higher levels introduce dictionary skills to help students become more independent learners.

▶ **Life-Skill Readings** Students will prepare for the reading by assessing their own knowledge and by making predictions about what they will read. Following the reading, they will do a variety of comprehension activities as well as expansion activities designed to help them relate the reading to their own lives.

▶ **Writing Practice** Students read a writing model and work through a series of pre-writing activities designed to facilitate their writing process. Their final task is to compose an original writing based on the previous model. Through the series, students progress from writing simple sentences to producing to complex paragraphs, and finally multi-paragraph writings.

▶ **Editing** Students self-correct their own work and then share with peers for more suggestions. Students complete each unit by writing a final draft.

▶ **Community Challenge** Each unit ends with a challenge that requires students to complete a community task related to the life-skill topic from the competency area that they have just worked with.

ACKNOWLEDGEMENTS

The author and publisher would like to thank the following reviewers:

Marti Estrin
Santa Rosa Junior College, Santa Rosa, CA

Lawrence Fish
Shorefront YM-YWHA English Learning Program, Brooklyn, NY

Kathleen Flynn
Glendale Community College, Glendale, CA

Kathleen Jimenez
Miami-Dade Community College, Miami, FL

Daniel Loos
Seattle Central Community College, Seattle, WA

Maya Redman
Miami-Dade Community College, Miami, FL

Eric Rosenberg
Bronx Community College, New York, NY

UNIT 1 **Talking with Others**

▶ GETTING READY

A **Look at the picture of Dalva with her class.**

B **Answer the questions. Check (✔) the boxes.**

1. How old is Dalva?

    ☐ 5 years old

    ☐ 25 years old

    ☑ 50 years old

2. Is she tall?

    ☐ Yes, she is.

    ☐ No, she isn't.

C **Answer the questions.**

1. How many people are in Dalva's class?

    _____ 10 pc. _____

2. How many people are in your class?

    _____ 12 Now _____

A **Answer the questions. Check (✔) the answers.**

1. Do you drive? ☐ Yes, I do. ☐ No, I don't.
2. Do you have a driver's license? ☐ Yes, I do. ☐ No, I don't.

B **Read Dalva's driver's license.**

DMV **CALIFORNIA** DMV
DRIVER LICENSE

Dalva Rodriguez
Address: 345 E. Birch Ave.
San Francisco   CA 94104

Sex: F   Hair: blond   Eyes: green
Height: 5' 6"   Weight: 121 lbs

Date of birth: 03-16-80

5'6" = 5 feet, 6 inches
121 lbs = 121 pounds

C **Write about Dalva.**

1. Name: _Dalva Rodriguez_

2. Height: _____

3. Weight: _____

4. Hair: _____

5. Eyes: _____

6. Age: _____

D **Write about yourself.**

1. Name: _____

2. Height: _____

3. Weight: _____

4. Hair: _____

5. Eyes: _____

6. Age: _____

A **Learn new words.**

She has *__curly__* hair.

He has *__short__* hair.

He is *__bald__*.

She has *__straight__* hair.

She has *__long__* hair.

He has *__wavy__* hair.

He is *__tall__*.
She is *__short__*.

The woman is *__old__*.

The man is *__young__*.

> ***average height*** =
>   not tall, not short
> ***average weight*** =
>   not thin, not heavy
> ***middle aged*** =
>   not young, not old

She is *__thin__*.

He is *__heavy__*.

B Read and circle.

1. Bill has (short)/ long hair.

2. Jan has <u>wavy / straight</u> hair.

3. Phillipe has <u>straight / curly</u> hair.

4. Jan is <u>young / old</u>.

5. Gilberto is <u>bald / has long hair</u>.

C Write the word.

1. Tien is (vyhae) _h_ _e_ _a_ _v_ _y_ .

2. Mary has (tritgahs) __ __ __ __ __ __ __ __ hair.

3. Chen has (luyrc) __ __ __ __ __ hair.

4. Tomek is very (hnit) __ __ __ __.

5. Piedra is a (nuogy) __ __ __ __ __ woman.

D Cross out the word that does not belong.

1. curly   straight   ~~tall~~

2. tall   heavy   short

3. bald   wavy   young

4. long   young   old

5. green   blue   old

E Look at the picture.

F Write sentences about Dalva's classmates. Use the words in the box.

bald	curly	heavy	long	old	short
straight	tall	thin	wavy	young	

EXAMPLE: _Dalva has long, wavy hair. She is young._

1. Steve _____

2. Lien _____

3. Anya _____

4. Mario _____

5. Kenji _____

6. Sung _____

7. Gilberto _____

8. Ahmed _____

9. Marie _____

G Talk to a partner. Talk about the people in the picture.

▶ **PRE-READING**

A Look at the picture.

B What words describe Dalva's mom? Check (✔) the boxes.

☐ bald	☐ curly	☐ straight	☐ wavy
☐ long	☐ blond	☐ brown	☐ black
☐ thin	☐ heavy	☐ tall	☐ short

C What words describe Dalva's brother? Check (✔) the boxes.

☐ bald	☐ curly	☐ straight	☐ wavy
☐ long	☐ blond	☐ brown	☐ black
☐ thin	☐ heavy	☐ tall	☐ short

► READING

D Read about Dalva.

> ## My Story
>
> My name is Dalva. I am tall and thin. I have long, wavy hair. My hair is blond and my eyes are green. I am 25 years old. I am from Brazil.

E Read about Dalva's mom and brother.

> My mom's name is Maria. She is tall and thin. She has long, curly hair. She has black hair and brown eyes. She is 50 years old. She is from Brazil.

> My brother's name is Alex. He is short and thin. He has long, straight hair. He has blond hair and green eyes. He is 30 years old. He is from Brazil.

► COMPREHENSION

F **Check (✔) the boxes.**

1. Maria has long hair. ☐ True ☐ False
2. Maria is heavy. ☐ True ☐ False
3. Maria has blue eyes. ☐ True ☐ False
4. Alex is 50 years old. ☐ True ☐ False
5. Alex is thin. ☐ True ☐ False
6. Alex has straight hair. ☐ True ☐ False

G **Complete the chart.**

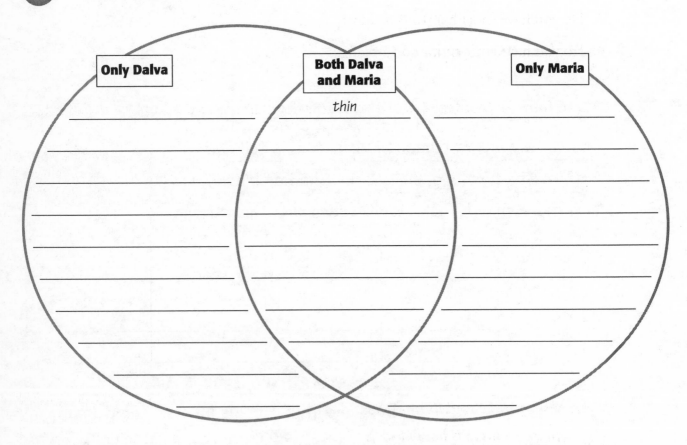

Only Dalva

Both Dalva and Maria

thin

Only Maria

H **Answer the questions.**

1. How old is Alex? _He is 30 years old._

2. Where is he from? _____

3. Does he have long hair or short hair? _____

4. Does he have curly hair or straight hair? _____

▶ **EXTENSION**

I **Answer the questions.**

1. How old are you? _____

2. Where are you from? _____

3. Do you have short hair or long hair? _____

4. Do you have straight hair or curly hair? _____

J **Talk to four classmates. Ask the questions from Exercise I. Complete the chart.**

Name	Age	Country	Short or long hair	Straight or curly hair

K **Write sentences about your classmates.**

EXAMPLE: _Vincent is from Mexico._

1. _____

2. _____

3. _____

4. _____

> **How old are you?**
> I'm 22 years old.
> **or**
> I'm sorry, that's personal.

▶ PREPARING

(A) Check (✔) the boxes.

1. I have ☐ long hair.
☐ short

2. I have ☐ straight hair.
☐ curly
☐ wavy

3. I have ☐ blue eyes.
☐ brown
☐ green

4. I am ☐ tall.
☐ short.

5. I am ☐ thin.
☐ heavy.

6. I am _____ years old.

(B) Write the missing words.

My name is _____. I have _____ ,

_____ hair. I have _____ eyes.

I am _____ and _____.

I am _____ years old. I am from _____.

▶ WRITING

C **Write about yourself. Use the examples on page 7 to help you.**

	My Story	

▶ EDITING

D **Check your writing.**

☐ Capital letters: My name is James.   my name is james.

☐ Periods: I am from Argentina.

E **Check a partner's writing.**

☐ Capital letters: My name is James.   my name is james.

☐ Periods: I am from Argentina.

F **Rewrite your story on another sheet of paper.**

A Write about five people in your neighborhood.

Name	Age	Hair	Weight	Height

B Do you have a driver's license? Complete the driver's license with your information.

Driver's License

Name: _____

Address: _____

Birth Date: _____ Age: _____

Weight: _____ Height: _____

Hair: _____ Eyes: _____

Your photo here

UNIT 2

Let's Go Shopping

▶ GETTING READY

A **Look at the picture of Roberto.**

Roberto

B **Answer the questions. Check (✔) the boxes.**

1. Where is Roberto?

   ☐ He is in a store.

   ☐ He is in a bank.

2. What does he want?

   ☐ clothes

   ☐ food

C **What clothes do you see in the picture? Write them down.**

_____

_____

_____

► READING CHALLENGE 1

A Answer the questions. Check (✔) the boxes.

1. Do you like shopping? ☐ Yes, I do. ☐ No, I don't.
2. Where do you buy clothes? _____

B Read the advertisement.

C Write about the advertisement.

1. How much are DVD players? ___*They are $59.*___

2. How much are shoes? _____

3. How much are shorts? _____

4. What costs $24? _____

5. What costs $78? _____

D Answer the questions.

1. Which things do you have? _____

_____

2. Which things do you want? _____

_____

A **Learn new words.**

My _**cell phone**_ is new.

I want a _**blouse**_.

I like my _**CD player**_.

I wear large _**socks**_.

I have black _**shoes**_.

He wants a
**video recorder**.

This is my _**skirt**_.

I like my _**dress**_.

I need a _**shirt**_.

I like this _**sweater**_.

I always wear _**pants**_.

I wear _**shorts**_.

I don't have a
**digital camera**.

I don't like
wearing _**hats**_.

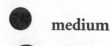 small

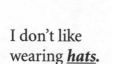 medium

large

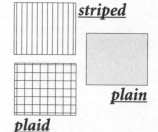

**striped**

**plain**

**plaid**

B Complete the chart with the words on page 16.

Clothing	Electronics
pants,	cell phone,

C Write the missing words.

1. Roberto has a **L** ___large___ ___digital camera___ .

2. Navra wants a _____ _____ .

3. Jane wants a _____ _____ .

4. Tien has a **M** _____ _____ .

5. I like wearing  _____ .

D Cross out the word that does not belong.

1. pants   shirt   blouse   ~~CD-player~~

2. skirt   tie   blouse   dress

3. CD-player   television   hat   camcorder

4. plaid   small   large   medium

E **Read and write the missing words.**

Salesperson: Can I help you?

Yusuf: Yes, I want a (irths) ____shirt____.

Salesperson: What size?

Yusuf: (Mdimue) _____.

Salesperson: How about this one?

Yusuf: No. I want (laidp) _____

or (tripsde) _____.

Salesperson: How about this one?

Yusuf: It looks nice. I'll take it! Thanks.

F **Talk to a partner. Practice the conversation.**

G **Look at the pictures. Write sentences.**

Natalia

Edgar

Bill

Joanne

1. Natalia wants ____a blouse____. She doesn't want ____a shirt____.

2. Edgar _____. He doesn't _____.

3. Bill _____. He _____.

4. Joanne _____. _____.

▶ **PRE-READING**

A Look at the advertisement.

B What can Roberto buy for Natalia's birthday? He has $50. Write sentences.

EXAMPLE: *He can buy a blouse and pants.*

1. _____
2. _____
3. _____
4. _____
5. _____
6. _____
7. _____
8. _____
9. _____
10. _____

► READING

C **Read about Roberto.**

Natalia's Birthday

I want to go shopping for my sister's birthday this weekend. Her name is Natalia. I like to shop at Karo's Department Store. My sister wants clothes. She wants sweaters and pants. She doesn't want socks or shoes. I have $50.

D **Read the sales slip.**

❈ **Karo's** ❈ **Department Store**		
1	Striped Sweater	$24.00
1	Blue Pants	$22.00
	Tax	$2.30
	TOTAL	$48.30

CUSTOMER COPY

► COMPREHENSION

E **Check (✔) the boxes.**

1. Roberto is buying a present for his mother. ☐ True ☐ False

2. Natalia is Roberto's sister. ☐ True ☐ False

3. Roberto doesn't like Karo's. ☐ True ☐ False

4. Natalia wants clothes for her birthday. ☐ True ☐ False

5. Natalia wants pants. ☐ True ☐ False

6. Natalia doesn't want socks. ☐ True ☐ False

7. Roberto has $100. ☐ True ☐ False

F **Answer the questions.**

1. What color pants does Roberto buy? _____

2. How many sweaters does Roberto buy? _____

3. How much is the tax? _____

4. How much is the total for the sweater, pants, and tax? _____

▶ **EXTENSION**

G **Answer the questions.**

1. What do you want for your birthday?

_____

2. What don't you want for your birthday?

_____

H **Talk to a student in your class. Put a check (✔) or cross (✘).**

Student name	Do you want...						
	a shirt?	a digital camera?	a hat?	a sweater?	a DVD player?		
Concepcion	✔	✘	✘	✔	✘		

> **Do you want . . .**
> ✔ Yes, I do.
> ✘ No, I don't.

I **Tell your class.**

EXAMPLE: Concepcion wants a shirt for her birthday.
She doesn't want a hat.

▶ WRITING CHALLENGE

▶ PREPARING

A Complete the chart about your family and friends.

Family member	Date of birth	Wants	Doesn't want
1. *Mom*	*3/8/45*	*sweater, pants*	*TV, cell phone*
2.			
3.			
4.			
5.			
6.			

B Write sentences. Use the information from Exercise A.

EXAMPLE: *My sister wants a blouse. She doesn't want a CD player.*

1. _____

2. _____

3. _____

4. _____

C Write. Use the example in Exercise C on page 19 to help you.

	_____'s Birthday	

D Complete a sales slip. Look back at page 18 for prices.

		Sales Slip
Quantity	**Item**	**Price**
	Tax	
	Total	

▶ EDITING

E **Check your writing.**

☐ Capital letters: ⒣er name is ⒩atalia.

☐ Periods: She wants clothes⊙

F **Check a partner's writing.**

☐ Capital letters: ⒣er name is ⒩atalia.

☐ Periods: She wants clothes⊙

G **Rewrite your paragraph on another sheet of paper.**

▶Community Challenge

A **Go to your local clothing store. Find clothes you like. Complete the chart.**

Item	Style	Size	Price
Shirts			
Pants			
Socks			
Sweaters			

B Write down three items you want. Search the Internet. Write the Web site name and price.

Item	Web site	Price

C Find an advertisement in a local newspaper like the one on page 18. Write down the special deals.

Item	Special deal
pants	save 50%

UNIT 3 Food

▶ GETTING READY

A Look at the picture of Yeshiareg.

B Answer the questions. Check (✔) the boxes.

1. Where is she?

   ☐ living room   ☐ bedroom   ☐ kitchen

2. What food do you see?

   ☐ eggs   ☐ apples   ☐ onions

   ☐ yogurt   ☐ celery   ☐ butter

A   **Answer the questions. Check (✔) the box.**

1. Do you cook?

☐ Yes, I do.

☐ No, I don't.

2. What do you cook?

_____

B   **Read the recipe.**

Baked Chicken

Ingredients	1 whole chicken	⅓ cup of butter
	3 slices of bread	2 eggs
	1 stalk of celery	½ tsp baking powder
	1 onion	2 cups milk

C   **Circle the ingredients.**

(eggs)	mustard	baking powder
onions	tomatoes	bread
ground beef	butter	carrots
celery	sugar	mayonnaise
chicken		

A **Learn new words.**

Spaghetti is easy to make.

I like *toast* for breakfast.

I love *chicken* and *French fries*.

This is a *can*.

I like *rice*.

These *tacos* are delicious!

Do you want *pancakes* for breakfast?

This is a *carton*.

You need lettuce for a *salad*.

I love *chocolate bars*.

Please buy some *fruit*.

These are *bottles*.

I eat *cereal* for *breakfast*.

I eat a *sandwich* for *lunch*.

I eat *steak* for *dinner*.

This is a *box*.

B Complete the chart.

Breakfast food	Lunch food	Dinner food
eggs		

C Write the missing words.

1. Can I have some (reclea) _c_ _e_ _r_ _e_ _a_ _l_ for breakfast please?

2. I'm having a chicken (sdwhcian) __ __ __ __ __ __ __ __ for lunch.

3. Do you want a (lsdaa) __ __ __ __ __ with your dinner?

4. My favorite breakfast food is (ggse) __ __ __ __ .

5. I have (kichenc) __ __ __ __ __ __ __ and French fries for dinner.

6. I don't like (oastt) __ __ __ __ __.

7. What do you eat for (nednir) __ __ __ __ __ __?

8. I like (cotsa) __ __ __ __ __ for dinner.

D Answer the questions about you. Write "Yes, I do" or "No, I don't."

1. Do you like spaghetti? —————————————————

2. Do you like salad? —————————————————

3. Do you like rice? —————————————————

4. Do you like tacos? —————————————————

5. Do you like chicken? —————————————————

6. Do you like eggs? —————————————————

E **Write the missing words.**

1. Open the _____carton_____ of milk.

2. Please buy a _____ of pickles.

3. We need a _____ of oil.

4. We need a _____ of soup.

F **Complete the chart. Use words from the box.**

| orange juice | eggs | soda | cookies | honey |
| wine | mustard | pasta | soup | cereal |

Carton	Box	Jar	Bottle	Can
	cookies			

▶ PRE-READING

A **Look at Yeshiareg's shopping list.**

Shopping list	
cereal	salad
fruit	yogurt
packet of rice	cheese
a pound of chicken	jar of honey
bottle of cola	carton of eggs

B **Answer the questions.**

1. What does she like for breakfast?

   _____

2. What does she like for dinner?

   _____

► **READING**

C Read about Yeshiareg.

My Eating Habits

My name is Yeshiareg. I'm from Ethiopia. I like to eat cereal for breakfast. I usually eat a green salad and fruit for lunch. I sometimes have baked chicken and vegetables for dinner. I drink a bottle of soda. My favorite food is yogurt. I don't like potatoes. Sometimes I eat at Mario's restaurant. I like the spaghetti there.

D Read about Kate and Silvia.

Food I Like to Eat

My name is Kate. I'm from the United States, but I like Asian food. I especially like Chinese food. My favorite restaurant is next to my house. I go there every night. I eat chicken or beef with rice. I eat a small breakfast every day, and I only eat a sandwich for lunch.

I Love to Eat

My name is Silvia. I'm from Cuba. I love to eat. It is important to eat good food. I drink a lot of water every day and exercise too. I eat a big breakfast. I like chicken for lunch and dinner. I have a chicken sandwich for lunch and baked chicken for dinner two times a week.

► COMPREHENSION

E **Check (✔) the boxes.**

1. Yeshiareg eats a small breakfast.   ☐ True   ☐ False
2. Yeshiareg likes fruit.   ☐ True   ☐ False
3. Kate likes Chinese food.   ☐ True   ☐ False
4. Kate eats a big breakfast.   ☐ True   ☐ False
5. Silvia doesn't drink water.   ☐ True   ☐ False
6. Silvia eats chicken a lot.   ☐ True   ☐ False

F **Complete the sentences. Check (✔) the boxes.**

1. Yeshiareg eats

   ☐ a small breakfast   ☐ a big breakfast   ☐ no breakfast
   ☐ a small lunch   ☐ a big lunch   ☐ no lunch
   ☐ a small dinner   ☐ a big dinner   ☐ no dinner

2. Kate eats

   ☐ a small breakfast   ☐ a big breakfast   ☐ no breakfast
   ☐ a small lunch   ☐ a big lunch   ☐ no lunch
   ☐ a small dinner   ☐ a big dinner   ☐ no dinner

3. Silvia eats

   ☐ a small breakfast   ☐ a big breakfast   ☐ no breakfast
   ☐ a small lunch   ☐ a big lunch   ☐ no lunch
   ☐ a small dinner   ☐ a big dinner   ☐ no dinner

G **Complete the chart.**

Yeshiareg likes to eat	Kate likes to eat	Silvia likes to eat

H Talk to a partner.

EXAMPLE:

Student A: *What does Kate eat for lunch?*

Student B: *She eats a sandwich.*

usually = on a normal day

▶ **EXTENSION**

I Talk to three students in your class. Complete the chart.

Student name	What do you usually eat for breakfast?	What do you usually eat for lunch?	What do you usually eat for dinner?
1.			
2.			
3.			

J Write sentences about the students in Exercise I.

EXAMPLE: *Mario eats cereal for breakfast.*

1. _____

2. _____

3. _____

4. _____

5. _____

6. _____

▶ WRITING CHALLENGE

▶ PREPARING

A Check (✔) what is true for you.

☐ I eat a big breakfast. ☐ I eat a big lunch. ☐ I eat a big dinner.

☐ I eat a small breakfast. ☐ I eat a small lunch. ☐ I eat a small dinner.

☐ I don't eat breakfast. ☐ I don't eat lunch. ☐ I don't eat dinner.

B What do you usually eat? Complete the chart.

For breakfast	For lunch	For dinner

C Write sentences about Exercise B.

EXAMPLE: _I eat eggs and orange juice for breakfast. I don't eat cereal._

1. _____

2. _____

3. _____

4. _____

5. _____

6. _____

D **What restaurants are near your home? Check (✔) the boxes.**

☐ Chinese   ☐ Japanese   ☐ Greek   ☐ Ethiopian

☐ Italian   ☐ Mexican   ☐ Thai   ☐ Brazilian

E **What is the name of your favorite restaurant?**

_____

► WRITING

F **Write about what you like to eat.**

	My Eating Habits	

► EDITING

G **Check your writing.**

☐ Capital letters: Ⓘeat a big breakfast.

☐ Periods: I eat a big breakfast⦿

H **Check a partner's writing.**

☐ Capital letters: Ⓘeat a big breakfast.

☐ Periods: I eat a big breakfast⦿

I **Rewrite your paragraph on another sheet of paper.**

A Plan a lunch at a restaurant with the class. Talk about the food on the menu.

B Imagine you are starting a new restaurant in your neighborhood. Plan the menu.

UNIT 4

Housing

▶ GETTING READY

A Look at the picture of Saud.

B Answer the questions.

1. Where is Saud?

_____

2. Why is he there?

_____

A **Answer the questions.**

1. Where do you live? _____

2. Do you live in a house or an apartment? _____

B **Read the classified advertisement.**

Homes for Rent and for Sale

| ★ House for Sale!
3 bdrms, 1 bath,
a/c, lge yard,
nr park: $125,000. | Apartment
for Rent ★
2nd flr, 1 bdrm,
1 bath, gas pd: $700. |
| Condominium for Sale!
2 bdrms, 2 baths, deck,
nr the university:
★ $98,000. | Mobile Home for Rent!
2 bdrms, 1 bath,
electric pd, backyard:
$350. ★ |

bdrm = bedroom, bath = bathroom
nr = near, a/c = air conditioning
pd = paid, lge = large, flr = floor

C **Complete the chart.**

Kind of home	Bedrooms	Bathrooms	$
1. House	3		$125,000
2. Condominium			
3. Apartment			
4. Mobile Home		1	

D **Which home do you think Saud will like? Circle.**

House   Condominium   Apartment   Mobile Home

A **Learn new words.**

| sofa | coffee table | armchair | rug | bed |

| lamp | dresser | picture | bathtub | toilet |

| sink | trash can | stove | refrigerator | microwave |

The cat is *on* the TV.

The cat is *under* the table.

The picture is *above* the sofa.

The cat is *between* the sofa and the armchair.

The cat is *next to* the chair.

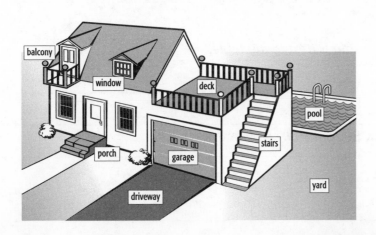

balcony
window
deck
pool
porch
garage
stairs
driveway
yard

B **Write the furniture in the rooms.**

Bedroom	Bathroom
bed	

Living room	Kitchen

C **Write sentences.**

EXAMPLE: (sofa, table) _The sofa is next to the table._

1. (cat, sofa) _____

2. (lamp, sofa) _____

3. (painting, sofa) _____

4. (rug, floor) _____

5. (sofa, table, lamp) _____

D Read. Circle *Yes* or *No*.

Homes for Rent and for Sale

★ House for Sale! 3 bdrms, 1 bath, a/c, lge yard, nr park: $125,000.	Apartment for Rent ★ 2nd flr, 1 bdrm, 1 bath, gas pd: $700.
Condominium for Sale! 2 bdrms, 2 baths, deck, nr the university: ★ $98,000.	Mobile Home for Rent! 2 bdrms, 1 bath, electric pd, backyard: $350. ★

1. The house has three bedrooms.   Yes   No

2. The house has a small yard.   Yes   No

3. The condominium is near the park.   Yes   No

4. The condominium has a deck.   Yes   No

5. The apartment has air conditioning.   Yes   No

6. The mobile home has one bathroom.   Yes   No

E Write the words.

Saud: How many (dbermoos)

_____ does it have?

Agent: Three.

Saud: Does it have (ira ditocnignoin)

_____?

Agent: Yes, it does.

Saud: Does it have a (ckde) _____

and a large (dyra) _____?

Agent: Yes, it does.

Saud: Is it near public transportation?

Agent: No, it isn't. It's near the (rkap) _____

F Talk to a partner. Practice the conversation.

▶ **PRE-READING**

A Look at Saud's new home.

> *live* and *lives*
> I *live* in a house.
> Saud *lives* in a house.

B What do you think about Saud's home? Check (✔) the boxes.

1. I think he lives in _____.

   ☐ a house   ☐ a condominium   ☐ an apartment   ☐ a mobile home

2. I think it has _____.

   ☐ one bedroom   ☐ two bedrooms   ☐ three bedrooms

   ☐ four bedrooms   ☐ five bedrooms

3. I think it has _____.

   ☐ one bathroom   ☐ two bathrooms   ☐ three bathrooms

4. I think it has _____.

   ☐ a garage   ☐ a swimming pool   ☐ a front yard

   ☐ a backyard   ☐ a porch   ☐ a deck

5. I think he lives near _____.

   ☐ a park   ☐ a school   ☐ a store

► READING

C Read about Saud's home.

> ### My Home
>
> My name is Saud. I live in a house. It has three bedrooms and one bathroom. I like my living room. There is a sofa between two end tables. There is also a coffee table and an armchair in my living room. My house has a pool and a deck. My house also has a front yard and a garage. I live near a park and a school. I like my home.

D Read about Carmen and Alexander.

> My Home
>
> My name is Carmen. I live in an apartment. My apartment has three bedrooms and two bathrooms. My home has air conditioning. I live near a school. I don't like my home. I want to move.

> My Home
>
> My name is Alexander. I live in a condominium. My condominium has two bedrooms and one bathroom. I like my kitchen. It has a large refrigerator. There is a balcony and a large front yard. I live near a supermarket. I like my home.

▶ COMPREHENSION

E **Check (✔) the correct answers about Saud.**

1. He lives in _____.

   ☐ a house   ☐ a condominium   ☐ an apartment   ☐ a mobile home

2. His home has _____.

   ☐ one bedroom   ☐ two bedrooms   ☐ three bedrooms

   ☐ four bedrooms   ☐ five bedrooms

3. His home has _____.

   ☐ one bathroom   ☐ two bathrooms   ☐ three bathrooms

4. His home has _____.

   ☐ a garage   ☐ a swimming pool   ☐ a front yard

   ☐ a backyard   ☐ a porch   ☐ a deck

5. He lives near _____.

   ☐ a park   ☐ a school   ☐ a store

F **Complete the chart.**

Name	Kind of home	No. of bedrooms	No. of bathrooms
Saud			
Carmen			
Alexander			

G **Answer the questions.**

1. Does Carmen's house have air conditioning? _____

2. Does she like her home? _____

3. What is Alexander's favorite room? _____

4. Does he have a small or large front yard? _____

5. Does he like his home? _____

H **Talk to a partner about Carmen's home.**

1. Does Carmen live in a house?

2. Does it have three bedrooms?

3. Does it have one bathroom?

4. Does it have air conditioning?

> **Questions**
> *Does he live* in a house?
> Yes, he does. / No, he doesn't.
> *Does it have* three bedrooms?
> Yes, it does. / No, it doesn't.

▶ **EXTENSION**

I **Check (✔) the boxes.**

1. I live in

☐ a house   ☐ a condominium   ☐ an apartment   ☐ a mobile home

2. It has

☐ one bedroom   ☐ two bedrooms   ☐ three bedrooms

☐ four bedrooms   ☐ five bedrooms

3. It has

☐ one bathroom   ☐ two bathrooms   ☐ three bathrooms

4. It has

☐ a garage   ☐ a swimming pool   ☐ a front yard

☐ a backyard   ☐ a porch   ☐ a deck

5. I live near

☐ a park   ☐ a school   ☐ a store

J **Talk to a partner.**

1. Do you live in a house? Do you live in an apartment?
2. How many bedrooms does it have?
3. How many bathrooms does it have?

▶ **PREPARING**

A **Answer the questions.**

1. What kind of home do you have (house, condominium, apartment, mobile home)?

    _____

2. How many bedrooms do you have? _____

3. How many bathrooms do you have? _____

4. What rooms do you like in your home?

    ☐ the kitchen

    ☐ the bedroom

    ☐ the living room

    ☐ the dining room

5. What furniture is in the room you like? _____

    _____

6. Do you want to move or do you like your home?

    ☐ I want to move.

    ☐ I like my home.

B **Write sentences about your home.**

1. It has _____

2. There is _____

3. I live near _____

4. I like _____

    _____

    _____

▶ WRITING

C **Write about your home. Use the examples on page 43 to help you.**

	My Home	

▶ EDITING

D **Check your writing.**

☐ Capital letters: Ⓘt has a balcony.

☐ Periods: There is a sofa in the living roomⓄ

E **Check a partner's writing.**

☐ Capital letters: Ⓘt has a balcony.

☐ Periods: There is a sofa in the living roomⓄ

F **Rewrite your paragraph on another sheet of paper.**

A Talk to a friend in your neighborhood.

1. What kind of home do you have?
2. How many bedrooms do you have?
3. How many bathrooms do you have?
4. What rooms do you like in your home?
5. What furniture is in the room you like?
6. Do you want to move or do you like your home?

B Complete the chart.

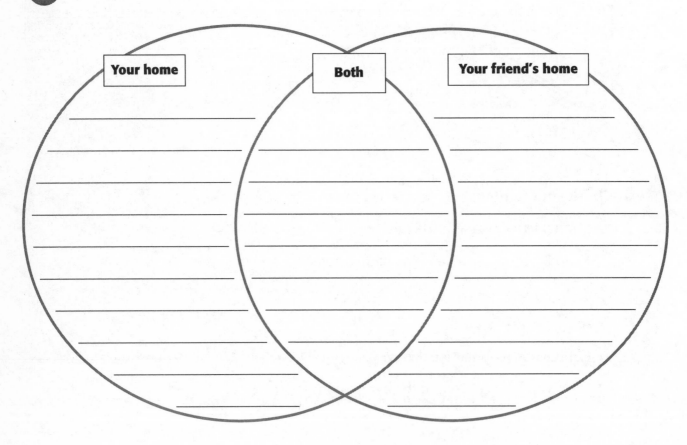

Your home

Both

Your friend's home

UNIT 5

Our Community

▶ **GETTING READY**

A Look at the picture of Duong Bui.

B Answer the questions. Check (✔) the boxes.

1. Where is Duong Bui?
   ☐ on Main Street   ☐ on Second Street
2. What buildings can you see?
   ☐ school   ☐ shops   ☐ bank
3. What is Duong Bui doing?
   ☐ He's going to school.   ☐ He's shopping.

A **Answer the questions. Check (✔) the boxes.**

1. Do you have hotels in your city? ☐ Yes, we do. ☐ No, we don't.
2. Do you have an airport? ☐ Yes, we do. ☐ No, we don't.
3. Where are the hotels and the airport? _____

B **Read.**

Alistair Hotel

2233 Broadway
Funnel
231-555-3215

The Alistair Hotel is easy to get to by air and car.

From the airport
Go west on Airport Way. Turn right on First. The hotel is on the corner of
First and Broadway.

By road
Take I-55. Take exit 15 to Funnel. Follow the signs to "downtown."

| Home |
| Rates |
| Vacancies |
| Directions |
| About Funnel |

C **Check (✔) the boxes.**

1. The hotel is in downtown Funnel. ☐ True ☐ False

2. Funnel doesn't have an airport. ☐ True ☐ False

3. The Alistair is an airport. ☐ True ☐ False

4. The Alistair is at 2333 Broadway. ☐ True ☐ False

D **Complete the chart about your community.**

Place	Street name
your school	
a supermarket	
a bank	

A Learn new words.

You mail letters at the **_post office_**.

You get money from a **_bank_**.

I am very sick. I need to go to the **_hospital_**.

You get aspirin from a **_pharmacy_**.

Police officers work at a **_police station_**.

Judges work in a **_courthouse_**.

We have an art **_museum_** in our town.

A **_library_** has lots of books.

turn left

turn right

go straight

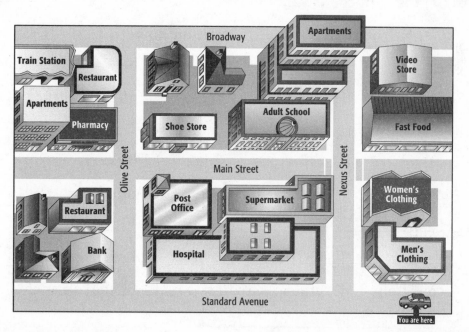

The bank is **_on_** Standard Avenue. The adult school is **_across from_** the supermarket.

The pharmacy is **_on the corner of_** Olive and Main Street. The apartments are **_around the corner_** from the adult school.

B **Read the map.**

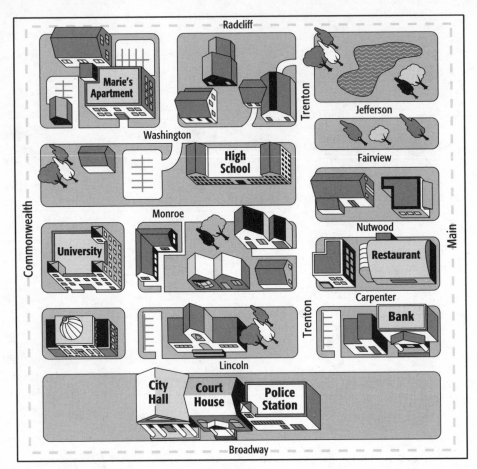

C **Check (✔) the correct answer.**

1. The City Hall office is _____ the courthouse.

   ☐ next to   ☐ on   ☐ in   ☐ between

   ☐ across from   ☐ around the corner   ☐ on the corner of

2. The university is _____ Commonwealth and Carpenter.

   ☐ next to   ☐ on   ☐ in   ☐ between

   ☐ across from   ☐ around the corner   ☐ on the corner of

3. The bank is _____ the restaurant.

   ☐ next to   ☐ on   ☐ in   ☐ between

   ☐ across from   ☐ around the corner   ☐ on the corner of

4. The police station is _____ Broadway.

   ☐ next to   ☐ on   ☐ in   ☐ between

   ☐ across from   ☐ around the corner   ☐ on the corner of

D **Write sentences about the map on page 52.**

1. _____ is around the corner from _____.

2. _____ is between _____

and _____.

3. _____ is next to _____.

4. _____ is across from _____.

E **You are on the corner of Broadway and Main. Check (✔) the answers.**

1. Go straight on Main. Turn left on Lincoln. It's on the right.

   ☐ the high school   ☐ Marie's Apartments   ☐ the bank

2. Go straight on Broadway. Turn right on Commonwealth. Turn right on Carpenter.

   It's on the left.

   ☐ the museum   ☐ the university   ☐ the police station

3. Go straight on Main. Turn left on Fairview. Turn right on Trenton. Turn left on

   Washington. It's on the left.

   ☐ the restaurant   ☐ the bank   ☐ the high school

4. Go straight on Broadway. It's between City Hall and the police station on

   the right.

   ☐ City Hall   ☐ the courthouse   ☐ the police station

F **Write the directions. You are on the corner of Broadway and Main.**

1. Please give me directions to the university.

   Go _____. Turn _____.

   Go three blocks. It's _____.

2. Please give me directions to City Hall.

   Go _____. It's _____.

3. Please give me directions to the high school.

   Go _____. Turn _____.

   Turn _____. Turn _____.

   It's _____.

► **PRE-READING**

A **Look at the map of Duong Bui's city.**

Welcome to Downtown Funnel

High School

Bank

City Hall

Main

Mall

First

Hotel

Second

Post Office   Motel

Tennis Courts

Third

Apartments

Broadway

Pool   Park

DMV

Adult School

Fast Food

Fast Food   Shoe Store   Gas Station

Hospital

Grand

Medical Center

Mobile Homes

Funnel —*a great community to live in!* **For information call: 555-234-2214**

B **Answer the questions about Funnel. Write complete sentences.**

1. How many fast-food restaurants are in Funnel?

    _____

2. How many schools are in Funnel? _____

3. What street is the DMV on? _____

4. What's next to the gas station? _____

5. Where are the apartments? _____

► READING

C Read Duong's letter.

August 21, 2005

Dear Mom,

　　I love my new home! I live in a beautiful neighborhood.

　　Funnel is an old city. I live in an apartment on Third Street. I work around the corner at the post office. The school is also close. It's on Grand Street. I like eating at the fast-food place next to the shoe store. The tennis courts are next to the post office. I play tennis every morning.

　　I hope you can visit me soon. There is a motel on the corner of my street. It's closed. You can stay at the hotel. It's across from the shopping mall. I know you love shopping!

See you soon!
Duong

► **COMPREHENSION**

D **Check (✔) the boxes.**

1. Duong lives in _____.

   ☐ a house   ☐ an apartment   ☐ a mobile home

2. Funnel is _____.

   ☐ a quiet city   ☐ a noisy city   ☐ an old city

3. Duong works _____.

   ☐ in a fast-food restaurant   ☐ in a hospital   ☐ at the post office

4. Duong likes to _____.

   ☐ go shopping   ☐ go swimming   ☐ play tennis

E **Answer the questions. Write the number on the map.**

1. Where does Duong live?
2. Where does he work?
3. Where does he go to school?
4. Where does he play tennis?
5. Where does he like to eat?

F **Write sentences.**

1. What street does Duong live on?

   _____

2. What building is across from his apartment?

   _____

3. Where does Duong work?

   _____

4. What does Duong like to do?

   _____

G **Answer the questions.**

1. Who is Duong writing to?

   _____

2. Is he sad?

   _____

3. Is he busy?

   _____

4. Does he like Funnel?

   _____

▶ **EXTENSION**

H **Talk to a classmate. Answer the questions.**

1. Where do you live?
2. What street do you live on?
3. Do you like where you live? Why?

▶ PRE-WRITING

(A) **Circle.**

1. I <u>love</u> / <u>like</u> / <u>don't like</u> my home.

2. I live in a <u>small</u> / <u>big</u> / <u>quiet</u> / <u>noisy</u> / <u>beautiful</u> neighborhood.

3. [*Your city*] is <u>a new</u> / <u>an old</u> city.

(B) **Answer the questions about you.**

1. What street do you live on?

   I live on _____

2. What do you live next to?

   I live next to _____

3. What do you live around the corner from?

   I live around the corner from _____

4. What do you live across from?

   I live across from _____

5. Where do you like to go?

   I like to go to _____

(C) **Answer the questions.**

1. Who will you write to?

   _____

2. What's the date today?

   _____

D Look at the parts of a letter.

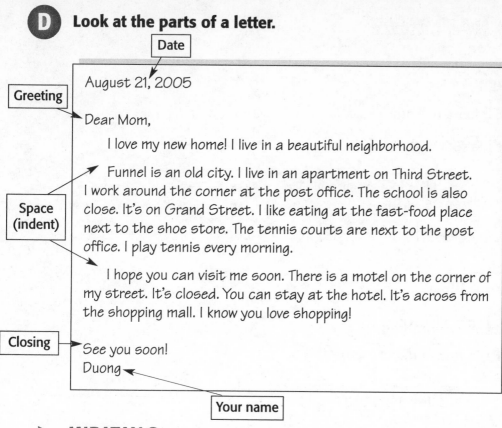

Date

August 21, 2005

Greeting

Dear Mom,

    I love my new home! I live in a beautiful neighborhood.

Space (indent)

    Funnel is an old city. I live in an apartment on Third Street. I work around the corner at the post office. The school is also close. It's on Grand Street. I like eating at the fast-food place next to the shoe store. The tennis courts are next to the post office. I play tennis every morning.

    I hope you can visit me soon. There is a motel on the corner of my street. It's closed. You can stay at the hotel. It's across from the shopping mall. I know you love shopping!

Closing

See you soon!
Duong

Your name

▶ WRITING

E Write a letter.

F **Check your writing.**

☐ Capital letters: I̶t has a balcony.

☐ Periods: There is a sofa in the living room.

☐ Indent:

> ○ I live in a small city. I live
> in Lansbury.

G **Check a partner's writing.**

☐ Capital letters: I̶t has a balcony.

☐ Periods: There is a sofa in the living room.

☐ Indent:

> ○ I live in a small city. I live
> in Lansbury.

H **Rewrite your letter on another sheet of paper.**

► **Community Challenge**

A **Give a partner directions to your home from your school.**

B **Describe your community to a partner.**

UNIT 6

Health and Fitness

▶ GETTING READY

A Look at the picture.

B Answer the questions. Check (✔) the boxes.

1. Where is John?
   ☐ at home
   ☐ at the doctor's

2. What is John's problem?
   ☐ He has a stomachache.
   ☐ He has a sore throat.

A **Answer the questions.**

1. Do you have a doctor? _____

2. When do you go to the doctor? _____

B **Read.**

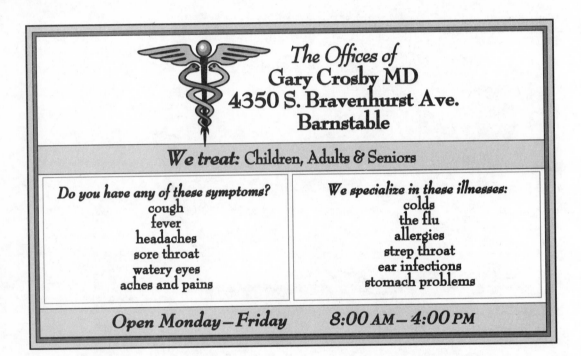

The Offices of
Gary Crosby MD
4350 S. Bravenhurst Ave.
Barnstable

We treat: Children, Adults & Seniors

Do you have any of these symptoms?
cough
fever
headaches
sore throat
watery eyes
aches and pains

We specialize in these illnesses:
colds
the flu
allergies
strep throat
ear infections
stomach problems

Open Monday—Friday   8:00 AM – 4:00 PM

C **Answer the questions.**

1. What is the doctor's name? _____

2. What is the address? _____

3. Does the doctor treat children? _____

4. What days is the office open? _____

Learn new words.

Symptoms and Illnesses

He has a ***sore throat***.
He has a ***runny nose***.
He has a ***fever***.

Take cough syrup
for a ***cough***.

He has a
stomachache.

My back hurts.
I have a ***backache***.

Remedies

Take ***aspirin*** when
you have a headache.

She needs a
throat lozenge for
her sore throat.

Cough syrup is
a medicine
for coughs.

Take an ***antacid***
for an upset
stomach.

Good Health Practices

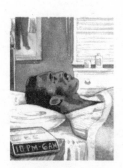

Some doctors say
we should ***exercise***
30 minutes a day.

We should ***drink***
a lot of water.

Some doctors say
to ***sleep*** eight hours
every night.

B **Write sentences.**

1. Your stomach hurts. You ___*have a stomachache.*___

2. Your head hurts. You _____

3. Your ear hurts. _____

4. Your back _____. _____

C **Write.**

Symptom	Remedy	Symptom	Remedy
1. sore throat		5. sneezing	
2. backache		6. fever	
3. stomachache		7. headache	
4. cough			

D **Write.**

1. He should take
_____ for a stomachache.

Should

I **should** take an aspirin.
He **should** take some antacid.

2. You should take
_____ for a cough.

3. I should take an aspirin for my _____.

4. She should take a _____ for a sore throat.

E **Complete the conversations.**

1. *Doctor:* What's the matter?

   Miguel: I have a bad (oughc) _ _ _ _ _ _ .

   Doctor: You should take some (ouchg yspru) _ _ _ _ _ _   _ _ _ _ _ _ .

2. *Doctor:* What's wrong?

   Nam: I have a (rose hrtaot) _ _ _ _   _ _ _ _ _ _ _ .

   Doctor: You should take a (hrtaot zgloene) _ _ _ _ _ _   _ _ _ _ _ _ _ .

3. *Doctor:* You don't look well.

   Timo: My head hurts. I have a (eahhcdea) _ _ _ _ _ _ _ _ .

   Doctor: You need an (spaniir) _ _ _ _ _ _ _ .

F **Practice the conversations with a partner.**

G **Check (✔) what you think are good health practices.**

☐ Walk one mile every day

☐ Eat a cheeseburger for lunch every day

☐ Drink a lot of water

☐ Sleep 12 hours every night

☐ Watch TV

☐ Exercise 30 minutes every day

▶ PRE-READING

A **What symptoms do people often have with a cold?**

☐ backache ☐ runny nose

☐ stomachache ☐ sore throat

☐ fever ☐ cough

☐ headache ☐ can't sleep

☐ feels tired ☐ sneezing

B **What are some remedies for John's symptoms?**

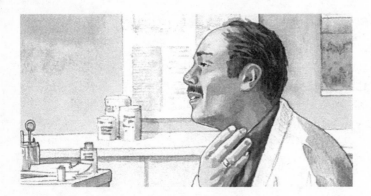

☐ He should take cough medicine.

☐ He should get some rest.

☐ He should take a throat lozenge.

☐ He should take an antacid.

☐ He should take an aspirin or other pain reliever.

☐ He should drink a lot of liquids.

► **READING**

C **Read about John.**

John's Health

John is sick. He is having many problems. Right now he has a sore throat. He also has a runny nose. The doctor says that John has a cold. John is confused because he had a cold two weeks ago, too. John thinks that he has other problems. He gets sick a lot. It is October now. John had the flu in July, a very bad stomachache in August, a cold in September, and now he is sick again. He didn't go to work 20 days this year, and now he has to miss work again. The doctor suggests that John take some medical tests to see if there are other problems.

D **Read about Miyuki.**

My Health

by Miyuki Tanaka

I am healthy. I eat well and rarely get sick. I was sick one time last year. I had a cold. I had a headache and a runny nose, and I was tired a lot. I had the cold for 10 days.

I exercise two times a day. I exercise in the morning for 20 minutes and I walk in the evening for 20 minutes every day. I drink a lot of water, take vitamins, and eat three meals a day. I think that I am very healthy.

► COMPREHENSION

E **Check (✔) the boxes.**

1. John is never sick. □ True □ False

2. John has a cold. □ True □ False

3. John is confused. □ True □ False

4. Miyuki exercises every day. □ True □ False

5. Miyuki doesn't drink water. □ True □ False

6. Miyuki eats four meals a day. □ True □ False

F **Complete the chart.**

John's symptoms	Miyuki's symptoms
1.	1.
2.	2.
	3.

G **What are the symptoms when you have a cold?**

Your cold symptoms

▶ **EXTENSION**

H **Talk to three students. Ask questions with** *how often . . . ?*

> **How often . . . ?**
> How often do you get a cold?
> I get a cold three times a year.
> I get a cold once a year.

I **Complete the graph.**

How many times a year	John	You	Student 1	Student 2	Student 3
5					
4					
3					
2					
1	once a year				

J **Write sentences.**

EXAMPLE: *John gets a cold once a year.*

1. _____

2. _____

3. _____

4. _____

▶ WRITING CHALLENGE

▶ PREPARING

Present	Past
I **have** a sore throat. He **has** a fever.	I **had** a sore throat. He **had** a fever.

A **Write sentences about your illnesses last year.**

EXAMPLE: _Last year I had a sore throat._

1. _____

2. _____

3. _____

4. _____

5. _____

B **Talk to a partner. Answer the questions.**

1. How often are you sick?
2. What illnesses do you get?
3. What are the symptoms?
4. Do you go to the doctor when you are sick?

C **Complete the sentences and check (✔) what is true for you.**

☐ I walk _____ mile(s) every day.

☐ I eat well.

☐ I drink a lot of water.

☐ I sleep _____ hours every night.

☐ I exercise _____ minutes every day.

☐ I take vitamins.

▶ WRITING

D Write about your health. Use the example in Exercise D on page 67.

	My Health	

▶ EDITING

E Check your writing.

☐ Capital letters: (I) am very healthy.

☐ Periods: I am very healthy(.)

☐ Indent:
(○) I am very healthy.

F Check a partner's writing.

☐ Capital letters: (I) am very healthy.

☐ Periods: I am very healthy(.)

☐ Indent:
(○) I am very healthy.

G Rewrite your paragraph on another sheet of paper.

A Go to your doctor's office. Ask for information on colds and flu. Find out remedies.

B Find out what rules your workplace has about taking "sick days."

C Use the Internet to find information on how to stay healthy. Make a list. Share your ideas in class.

D How do you get to your doctor's office? Use the vocabulary from Unit 5.

Doctor's name	Address and phone number	Directions

Working on It

▶ GETTING READY

A **Look at the picture of Kristina.**

B **Answer the questions.**

1. What is Kristina's job?

   _____

2. Where does she work?

   _____

A **Answer the questions.**

1. Do you have a job? _____

2. What is your job? _____

B **Read**

> **Employee Evaluation Form**
>
> **Date:** January 15   **Name:** Kristina Perez
> **Company:** Rodman's Market   **Position:** Cashier
>   **Supervisor:** Esther Landi
>
> **Punctuality** (comes to work on time):
> (Needs improvement)   Good   Superior
>
> **Appearance** (professional dress and grooming):
> Needs improvement   Good   (Superior)
>
> **Follows instructions:**
> Needs improvement   (Good)   Superior
>
> **Helps others:**
> Needs improvement   Good   (Superior)
>
> **Has a positive attitude:**
> Needs improvement   Good   (Superior)
>
> **Signed:** Esther Landi

C **Check (✔) the boxes.**

1. Who is the evaluation about?

   ☐ Esther Landi   ☐ Rodman's Market   ☐ Kristina Perez

2. Does she come on time every day?

   ☐ Yes   ☐ No

3. Does she have a positive attitude?

   ☐ Yes   ☐ No

4. Does she help others?

   ☐ Yes   ☐ No

A Learn new words.

A *cashier* helps customers.

A *bus driver* drives a bus.

A *custodian* cleans offices.

A *doctor* helps sick people.

A *teacher* teaches students.

A *mechanic* fixes cars.

A *nurse* helps sick people.

A *salesperson* sells things.

A *police officer* protects people.

A *server* serves food in a restaurant.

An *office worker* answers phones.

A *student* learns at school.

B **Write.**

1. A _____ fixes cars.

2. _____ take care of people.

3. An _____ answers phones.

4. A _____ cleans offices.

C **Answer the questions. Circle.**

1. Does a teacher serve food in a restaurant?   **Yes**   **(No)**

2. Does an office worker answer the phones?   **Yes**   **No**

3. Does a cashier treat patients?   **Yes**   **No**

4. Does a police officer work in a hospital?   **Yes**   **No**

5. Does a custodian clean offices?   **Yes**   **No**

D **Write the missing words.**

1. My friend works in a restaurant. He's a (verser) __ __ __ __ __ __ .

2. A (olpcei efiforc) __ __ __ __ __ __ __ __ __ __ __ __ __ __ protects people.

3. A (sernu) __ __ __ __ __ helps sick people.

4. My brother is at medical school. He wants to be a (torcod) __ __ __ __ __ __ .

5. A (sosslapreen) __ __ __ __ __ __ __ __ __ __ __ sells things.

E Write sentences.

Now	Before
	server
	nurse
	custodian
	student

	Now	Before
1.	*He is a bus driver.*	*He was a server.*
2.		
3.		
4.		

F Write sentences.

EXAMPLE: (*police officer*) *I was a police officer.*

  (*protect*) *I protected people.*

1. (office worker) *She*
   (answer)
2. (cashier) *He*
   (help)
3. (mechanic) *She*
   (fix)
4. (student) *They*
   (learn)

The Simple past - regular verbs

I **protect** people. = I **protected** people.

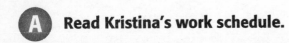

▶ READING CHALLENGE 2

▶ PRE-READING

A Read Kristina's work schedule.

Sunday	Monday	Tuesday	Wednesday	Thursday	Friday	Saturday
No work	No work	Work 8A.M.–3P.M.	Work 8A.M.–3P.M.	Work 3P.M.–10P.M.	Work 3P.M.–10P.M.	Work 8A.M.–3P.M.

B Write the answers.

1. What days does Kristina work?

   _____

2. What time does she work on Thursday?

   _____

3. What days doesn't she work?

   _____

C Check (✔) what you think is true about Kristina.

☐ She doesn't like her job.   ☐ She was a cashier.

☐ She likes her job.   ☐ She was a salesperson.

☐ She is a cashier.   ☐ She was a mechanic.

☐ She is a salesperson.   ☐ She was a doctor.

☐ She is a mechanic.   ☐ She is from Cuba.

☐ She is a doctor.   ☐ She is from Chile.

► READING

D Read about Kristina's work experience. Does she like her job?

My Work

My name is Kristina. I'm from Cuba. I am a cashier at Rodman's Market in Yorba. I work from 8:00 A.M. to 5:00 P.M. Tuesday through Saturday. I like my job, but I don't like working on Saturdays. I collect money for groceries and I give change. I started my job in 2003. Before this job, I was a salesperson in Cuba. I sold radios and televisions.

E Read about other people.

My Story

My name is Maritza. I'm a homemaker. I have three children, and I work very hard. I do the laundry, make dinner for the family, and teach my children many important things. I like the work. My husband, Ernesto, is a lawyer. He works ten hours a day, Monday through Saturday. He likes his job. He is a hard worker, and works well with other people. Before this job, he was a restaurant supervisor. He wrote evaluations about other employees and worked in a team.

My Story

My name is Gilberto. I work as a nurse at Bowman Memorial Hospital. The hospital serves a large community. I started working at the hospital last year. I really like my job. I take care of people and help doctors. I also have very good benefits. I get two weeks vacation every year. I like the patients, but the job is very difficult. Before this job, I went to nursing school. I never had a job in Cuba.

F **Check (✔) the boxes.**

1. Kristina is a salesperson.   ☐ True   ☐ False

2. Kristina doesn't like her job.   ☐ True   ☐ False

3. Kristina works on Saturday.   ☐ True   ☐ False

4. Gilberto doesn't have a job.   ☐ True   ☐ False

5. Gilberto started working at the hospital last year.   ☐ True   ☐ False

6. Maritza teaches her children.   ☐ True   ☐ False

G **Complete the chart.**

Name	Job	Likes job?	Job before
Kristina	*cashier*		
Gilberto			*student*
Maritza			
Ernesto		*yes*	

► EXTENSION

H **Write.**

EXAMPLE:

What does Kristina do?   She is a cashier.
Does she like her job?   Yes, she does.
What was her job before?   She was a salesperson.
What did she do?   She sold televisions and radios.

1. What does Gilberto do?

_____

2. Does he like his job?

_____

3. What was his job before?

_____

4. What did he do?

_____

5. What does Ernesto do?

_____

6. Does he like his job?

_____

7. What was his job before?

_____

8. What did he do?

_____

 Talk to a classmate. Ask the questions.

1. What do you do?
2. Where do you work?
3. Do you like your job?
4. What do you do in your job?
5. What did you do before?
6. Where did you work?
7. What did you do at your job?

A **Answer the questions. Write sentences.**

1. What is your job?

   I'm a _____

2. Where do you work?

   I work at _____

3. Do you like your job?

   _____

4. What do you do in your job?

   _____

B **Write your work schedule.**

Sunday	Monday	Tuesday	Wednesday	Thursday	Friday	Saturday

C **Answer the questions. Write sentences.**

1. What was your job?

   I was a _____

2. Where did you work?

   I worked at _____

3. What did you do at your job?

   _____

D Write about your jobs or work experience.

	My Work Experience	

E Write about a family member's jobs and experience. (husband, sister, brother, father, mother, etc.)

F **Check your writing.**

☐ Capital letters: (M)y name is (K)ristina.

☐ Periods: I'm from Cuba(.)

☐ Indent:

> (○) My name is Kristina. I'm
> from Cuba.

G **Check your partner's writing.**

☐ Capital letters: (M)y name is Kristina.

☐ Periods: I'm from Cuba(.)

☐ Indent:

> (○) My name is Kristina. I'm
> from Cuba.

H **Rewrite your paragraphs on another sheet of paper.**

▶ Community Challenge

A **Who works in your community? How do you contact them if there's a problem?**

Service	Job	Phone number
ambulance		
fire		
police		
trash collection		
mail delivery		

B **Talk to other people in your community. Ask them the questions on page 81.**

UNIT 8

People and Learning

▶ GETTING READY

A Look at the picture of Lien.

B Answer the questions. Check (✔) the boxes.

1. Where is Lien?
   - ☐ at school
   - ☐ at home

2. What is in her hand?
   - ☐ a shopping list
   - ☐ a diploma

A **Answer the questions.**

1. What is the name of your school? _____

2. Do you want to get a diploma? _____

B **Read about Amal's goals.**

Educational goals	Work goals
• Get a high school diploma • Go to adult school • Go to college	• Get a part-time job • Be a computer technician

C **Check (✔) the boxes.**

1. Amal doesn't want to get a diploma. ☐ True ☐ False

2. He wants to go to college. ☐ True ☐ False

3. He wants to be a nurse. ☐ True ☐ False

4. One of his educational goals is to go to adult school. ☐ True ☐ False

5. One of his work goals is to get a part-time job. ☐ True ☐ False

D **Answer the questions.**

1. What are your educational goals?
2. What job do you want to do in five years time?

A Learn new words.

Organize your
notebook.

Write your ideas
in a *journal*.

I want to get a high
school *diploma*.

I want to go to *trade school*
and learn carpentry.

I have a study *schedule*.

be		
Subject	**Verb**	**Example sentence**
I	am	I am from Mexico.
you	are	You are married.
he, she, it	is	She is 30 years old.
we	are	We are friends.
they	are	They are students.

I study *grammar*.

I practice *teamwork*
in class.

I have a *goal*. I want
to learn English.

---

organize — to put in order

study — to work to learn

practice — to do something lots of times to get it right

help — to aid, assist, or support

B **Read the paragraph. <u>Underline</u> the words.**

journal	trade school
~~goals~~	high school diploma

My name is Ana. I have many <u>goals</u>. First I want to learn English. I read every day for three hours. I write in a journal at night. I want to get a high school diploma. Then I want to go to a trade school and learn about computers. I want to get a full-time job in a big company when I finish school.

C **Write sentences about Ana from Exercise B. Use *want to*.**

Future with *want to*		
I	**want** **to** go	to college.
she	**wants** **to** get	a high school diploma.

1. *She wants to learn English.*
   _____

2. She _____

3. _____

4. _____

D **Read the paragraph about Omar. <u>Underline</u> the words.**

journal	grammar	~~goals~~
diploma	notebook	schedule

Future with *will*		
I	**will**	study	every day.
He	**will**	keep	his goals.

I study every day. I have a study schedule. In the summer, I will study one hour in the morning and one hour in the evening every day. I will study grammar for 30 minutes in the morning and watch TV in English for 30 minutes. In the evening, I will write in my journal and listen to the radio. I will keep my <u>goals</u> and write in a notebook. I want to get a high school diploma in three years.

E Write sentences about the paragraph in Exercise E. Use *will*.

1. _He will study one hour in the morning._

2. _____

3. _____

4. _____

F Talk to classmates. Complete the chart.

Student name	Do you have a study schedule?	Do you write in a journal?	Do you organize your notebook?

▶ PRE-READING

A **Look at Lien's goals.**

Educational goals	Work goals
• go to adult school and learn English • go to nursing school	• get a part-time job • get a job as a nurse

B **What do you think Lien's life goals are? Write sentences.**

1. *She wants to learn English.*

2. _____

3. _____

4. _____

C **Look at Lien's journal entries.**

June 2nd		June 3rd	
New Words:	video store, DVD, checkout counter	**New Words:**	stamps, letter opener, tape
Practice:	I wrote a letter to a friend.	**Practice:**	I talked to the man at the post office.
Book Work:	I studied pages 30-36 in my book.	**Book Work:**	I studied pages 41-46 in my book.
Listening:	I listened to the radio for 30 minutes in English.	**Listening:**	I listened to the radio for 30 minutes in English.
Writing:	I wrote in my journal.	**Writing:**	I wrote in my journal and wrote a letter.

D **What do you think Lien's study goals are? Complete the sentences.**

1. She wants to listen to the radio _____ minutes every day.

2. She wants to write in a _____ every day.

3. She wants to _____ pages in her book.

► READING

E Read about Lien's goals.

My Educational and Work Goals

My name is Lien. I have important goals. I want to learn English and get a high school diploma. English is difficult for me. I study every day. After I learn English and get a high school diploma, I will go to nursing school. The school will help me get a job at a hospital. Then I want to get married and have a big family.

F Read about Lien's study goals.

My Study Goals

I want to get my high school diploma. First I need to learn English. I will study every day. I want to learn three new words a day. I also want to study one lesson in the book every week. I think it is difficult, but I need to learn quickly so I can speak more. I will write in my journal and listen to the radio every day.

► COMPREHENSION

G Check (✔) the boxes.

1. Lien wants a high school diploma. ☐ True ☐ False
2. Lien wants to work in a post office. ☐ True ☐ False
3. Lien wants to get married. ☐ True ☐ False
4. Lien wants to study three lessons in the book every day. ☐ True ☐ False
5. Lien wants to learn 10 new words every day. ☐ True ☐ False
6. Lien wants to watch TV at night. ☐ True ☐ False

H Put the events in order for Lien.

____ get a high school diploma

____ get a job in a hospital

____ get married

____ go to nursing school

____ have a big family

__1__ learn English

1. _learn English_ _____

2. _____

3. _____

4. _____

5. _____

6. _____

I Check (✔) the boxes.

1. How many lessons does Lien want to study every week?
   ☐ one   ☐ two   ☐ three

2. How often does she want to listen to the radio?
   ☐ every month   ☐ every week   ☐ every day

3. How often does she want to write in a journal?
   ☐ every month   ☐ every week   ☐ every day

4. How many new words does she want to learn every day?
   ☐ three   ☐ five   ☐ nine

▶ EXTENSION

J Complete the sentences about you.

1. I want to study _____ lessons every week.

2. I want to listen to radio _____ times a week in English.

3. I want to write in a journal _____ times every week.

4. I want to learn _____ new words every week.

K **Talk to four classmates and complete the chart.**

Names	How many lessons do you want to study every week?	How many times do you want to listen to the radio every week?	How many times do you want to write in a journal every week?	How many new words do you want to learn every week?
Me				
My partner				

L **How are you and your partner the same and different?**

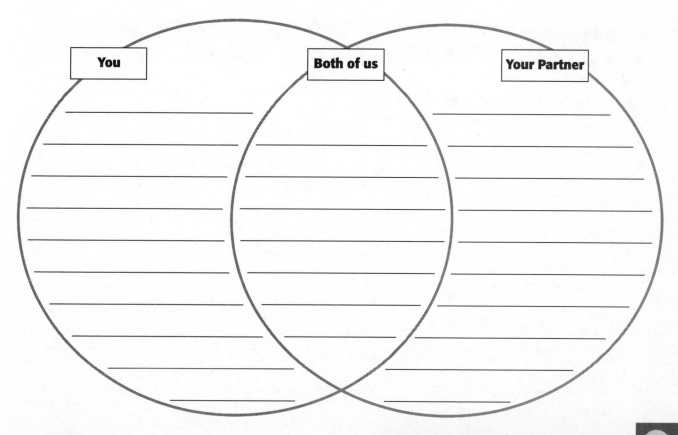

You · Both of us · Your Partner

▶ PREPARING

A Answer the questions. Write sentences.

1. Do you want to go to college?

   _____

2. What do you want to do when you learn English?

   _____

3. Do you want to get a high school diploma?

   _____

4. What kind of job do you want?

   _____

B Complete the chart.

My educational goals	My work goals

▶ **WRITING**

C Write about your educational and work goals. Use the example on page 91.

	My Educational and Work Goals	

D Write about your study goals. Use the example on page 91.

	My Study Goals	

E **Check your writing.**

☐ Capital letters: (M)y name is (L)ien.

☐ Periods: I have important goals(.)

☐ Indent:

> ◯ My name is Lien. I have
> important goals.

F **Check your partner's writing.**

☐ Capital letters: (M)y name is (L)ien.

☐ Periods: I have important goals(.)

☐ Indent:

> ◯ My name is Lien. I have
> important goals.

G **Rewrite your paragraphs on another sheet of paper.**

▶ Community Challenge

Talk to someone with a college degree in your neighborhood (like your doctor). Ask questions.

1. Do you like your job?
2. How many years did you go to college?
3. What is your first language?
4. Was school difficult for you?

APPENDIX

▶ VOCABULARY LIST

Unit 1
curly
bald
straight
long
wavy
tall
short
thin
young
heavy
old
average height
average weight
middle aged

Unit 2
cell phone
blouse
CD-player
socks
shoes
video recorder
skirt
dress
shirt
sweater
pants
shorts
digital camera
hats
small
medium
large
plaid
striped
plain

Unit 3
spaghetti
toast
chicken
french fries
can
rice
tacos
pancakes
carton
salad
chocolate bars
fruit
bottle
cereal
breakfast
sandwich
lunch
steak
dinner
box

Unit 4
sofa
coffee table
armchair
rug
bed
lamp
dresser
painting
bathtub
toilet
sink
trash can
oven
refrigerator
microwave

on
under
above
between
next to
balcony
window
deck
pool
stairs
yard
garage
driveway
porch

Unit 5
post office
bank
hospital
pharmacy
police station
courthouse
museum
library
turn left
turn right
go straight
on
across from
on the corner of
around the corner

Unit 6
sore throat
runny nose
fever
cough

stomachache
backache
aspirin
throat lozenge
cough syrup
antacid
exercise
drink
sleep

Unit 7
cashier
bus driver
custodian
doctor
teacher
mechanic
nurse
salesperson
police officer
server
office worker
student

Unit 8
notebook
journal
diploma
trade school
schedule
grammar
teamwork
goal
organize
study
practice
help

▶ IRREGULAR VERB FORMS

be	was	hear	heard
become	became	hide	hid
begin	began	hit	hit
blow	blew	keep	kept
break	broke	know	knew
bring	brought	lead	led
build	built	leave	left
buy	bought	lose	lost
catch	caught	make	made
choose	chose	meet	met
come	came	pay	paid
cut	cut	put	put
do	did	run	ran
drink	drank	say	said
drive	drove	see	saw
eat	ate	send	sent
fall	fell	sleep	slept
feel	felt	speak	spoke
fight	fought	spend	spent
find	found	take	took
fly	flew	teach	taught
forget	forgot	tell	told
get	got	think	thought
give	gave	understand	understood
go	went	wear	wore
grow	grew	win	won
have	had	write	wrote

▶ USEFUL WORDS

Cardinal numbers

1	one
2	two
3	three
4	four
5	five
6	six
7	seven
8	eight
9	nine
10	ten
11	eleven
12	twelve
13	thirteen
14	fourteen
15	fifteen
16	sixteen
17	seventeen
18	eighteen
19	nineteen
20	twenty
21	twenty-one
30	thirty
40	forty
50	fifty
60	sixty
70	seventy
80	eighty
90	ninety
100	one hundred
1000	one thousand
10,000	ten thousand
100,000	one hundred thousand
1,000,000	one million

Ordinal numbers

first	1st
second	2nd
third	3rd
fourth	4th
fifth	5th
sixth	6th
seventh	7th
eighth	8th
ninth	9th
tenth	10th
eleventh	11th
twelfth	12th
thirteenth	13th
fourteenth	14th
fifteenth	15th
sixteenth	16th
seventeenth	17th
eighteenth	18th
nineteenth	19th
twentieth	20th
twenty-first	21st

Days of the week

Sunday
Monday
Tuesday
Wednesday
Thursday
Friday
Saturday

Seasons

winter
spring
summer
fall

Months of the year

January
February
March
April
May
June
July
August
September
October
November
December

Write the date

April 5, 2004 = 4/ 5/ 04

Temperature chart

Degrees Celsius (ºC) and
Degrees Fahrenheit (ºF)

100ºC	212ºF
30ºC	86ºF
25ºC	77ºF
20ºC	68ºF
15ºC	59ºF
10ºC	50ºF
5ºC	41ºF
0ºC	32ºF
−5ºC	23ºF

Weights and measures

Weight:
1 pound (lb.) = 453.6 grams (g)
16 ounces (oz.) = 1 pound (lb.)
1 pound (lb.) = .45 kilogram (kg)

Liquid or Volume:
1 cup (c.) = .24 liter (l)
2 cups (c.) = 1 pint (pt.)
2 pints = 1 quart (qt.)
4 quarts = 1 gallon (gal.)
1 gallon (gal.) = 3.78 liters (l)

Length:
1 inch (in. or ″) = 2.54 centimeters (cm)
1 foot (ft. or ′) = .3048 meters (m)
12 inches (12″) = 1 foot (1′)
1 yard (yd.) = 3 feet (3′) or 0.9144 meters (m)
1 mile (mi.) = 1609.34 meters (m) or 1.609 kilometers (km)

Time:
60 seconds = 1 minute
60 minutes = 1 hour
24 hours = 1 day
28–31 days = 1 month
12 months = 1 year

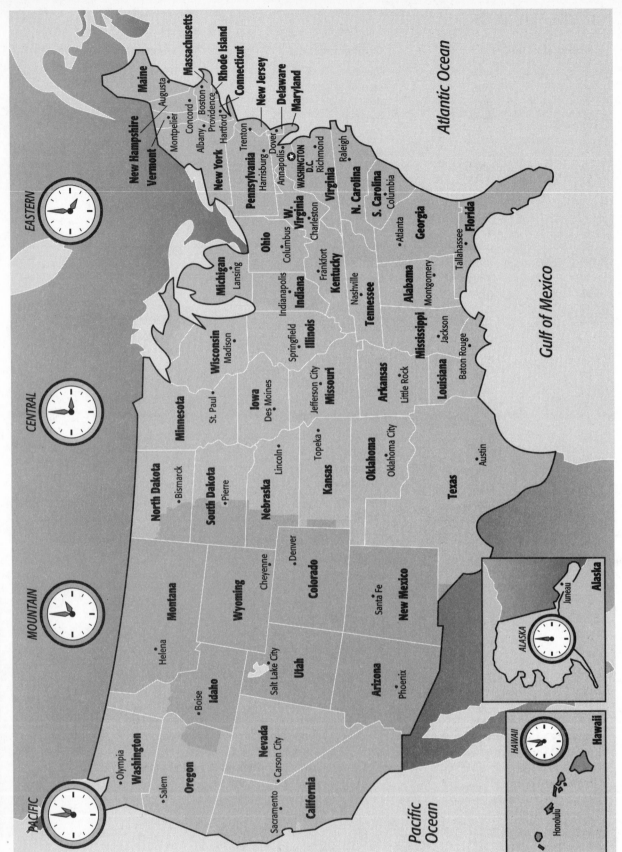